Recharging

Recharging
Recharging
Recharging

This Is Why You SLEEP

Dana Peabody

An imprint of PHOENIX International Publications, Inc.

Artwork © Shutterstock 2025 AYO Production; Pixoode; Shyamalamuralinath; Davidenco; creative_chieps; vesta2k; Iconic Bestiary; Zdenek Sasek; Rawpixel.com; Brocreative; svtdesign; Gatot Adri; Krakenimages.com; Sorapop Udomsri; Pressmaster; Streamlight Studios; nuwatphoto; Chz_mhOng; Nick Fedirko; Ka Han; robuart; CGN089; aomvector; LeManna; sirtravelalot; Zdan Ivan; Kasefoto; Mr.Karan Nandee; Mulad Images; New Africa; fizkes; Tarasyuk Igor; Retouch man

Published by Sequoia Kids Media,
an imprint of Sequoia Publishing & Media, LLC

Sequoia Publishing & Media, LLC,
a division of Phoenix International Publications, Inc.

8501 West Higgins Road, Chicago, Illinois 60631
34 Seymour Street, London W1H 7JE
Heimhuder Straße 81, 20148 Hamburg

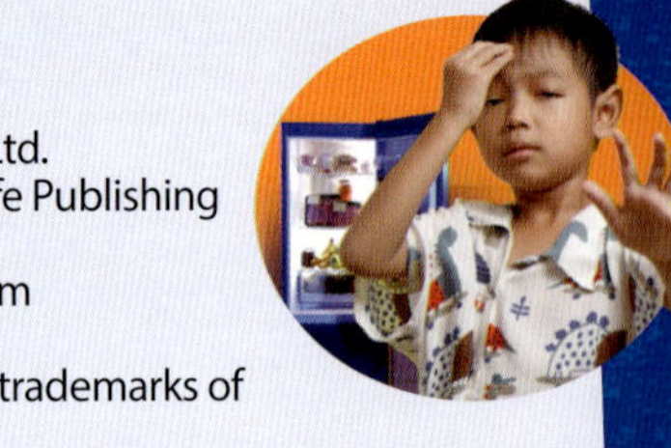

CustomerService@PhoenixInternational.com

www.PhoenixInternational.com

Library of Congress Control Number: 2024952390

ISBN: 979-8-7654-1133-9

This Is Why You SLEEP

Table of Contents

Bold words are explained in the glossary.

Are you Feeling Tired?

Is it getting late? Do you feel sleepy and want to go to bed? Most people get tired in the evenings.

It looks like you need a good night's rest!

Throughout the day, our bodies and minds have lots of important jobs to do, such as using our **muscles** or learning new things. That's a lot of work!

Yawning

Sometimes we yawn when we are tired and sleepy. Scientists aren't exactly sure why we yawn. At first, they thought it was to get more **oxygen** into our bodies, but this wasn't true.

Have you ever noticed that yawns are contagious? When one person yawns, a person near them will probably yawn too.

Nobody really knows why yawns are contagious! But you want to yawn right now, don't you?

Going to Bed

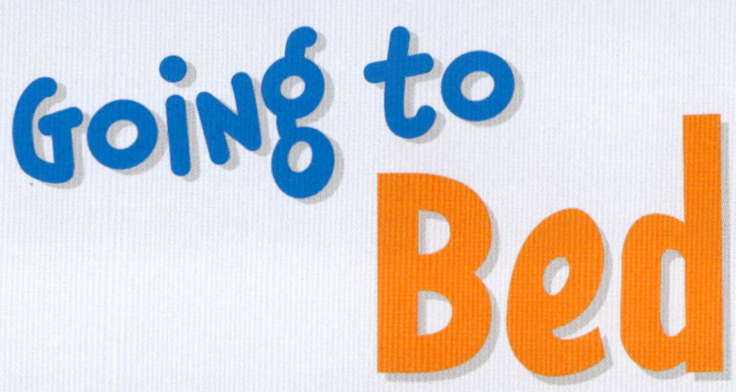

There are certain things you can do before you even get into bed to help you get a better night's sleep. Here are a few examples.

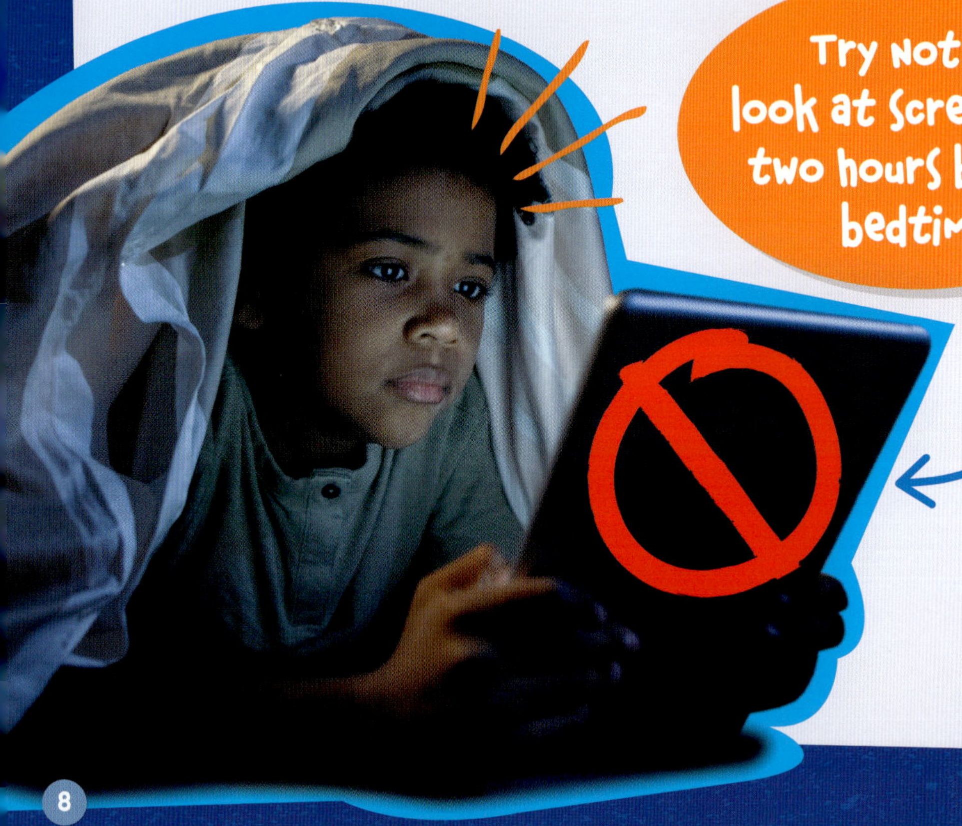

Try not to look at screens for two hours before bedtime.

All these things should help you have a long and peaceful night's sleep.

Sleep Phases

As you sleep, you go through lots of different phases.

PHASE 1:

You are barely asleep and can easily wake up, sometimes with a **SUDDEN JERK**. Your eyes may be slightly open.

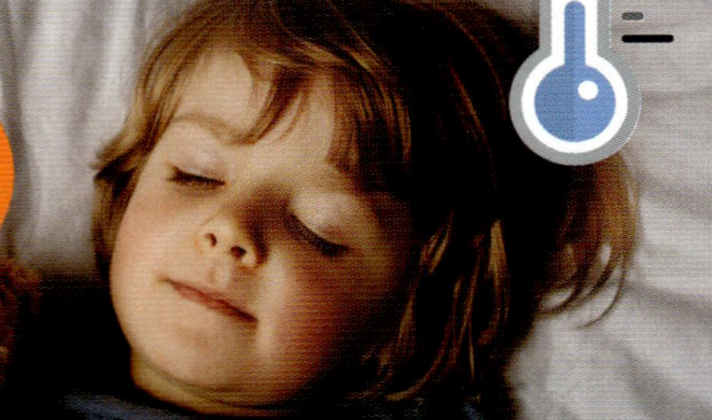

PHASE 2:

This is a slightly deeper phase of sleep and your body **temperature** begins to drop.

PHASE 3:

This is the deepest phase of sleep. It is when the body **repairs** and GROWS while also strengthening the **immune system**.

PHASE 4:

This phase of sleep is known as rapid eye movement (REM) sleep. This is when you have **vivid** dreams or nightmares.

The different stages of sleep can come in different orders at different times of the night.

Snoring and Drooling

Sometimes when we sleep, we can drool all over our pillows.

Our bodies are always making saliva (spit). When awake, we just swallow the saliva. But when we are asleep, the muscles in our face relax and the saliva leaks out.

Snoring also happens because our facial muscles are relaxed. Sometimes your mouth, throat, and airways in your nose **vibrate** as you breathe.

These vibrations can make very loud noises as you breathe in and out!

Dreams

We mostly dream in phase four of sleep. Our brains almost act as if we are awake, but without our bodies moving.

Most of the time we won't remember a dream unless we are woken up in the middle of it.

Sometimes dreams don't make sense, but they can help us understand what is happening in our lives.

Nightmares

Nightmares are dreams that might scare us. They might wake us up screaming or sweating.

Scientists think we have nightmares because of **evolution**.

Nightmares helped us to be ready for any scary things out there!

We can have nightmares about lots of different things. Sometimes they might be about things that are happening in real life.

Sleepwalking

When a sleeping person walks around or acts as if they are still awake, it is called sleepwalking. Sleepwalking usually takes place in phase three of sleep and can include talking or walking around.

It may seem scary, but sleepwalking is completely normal.

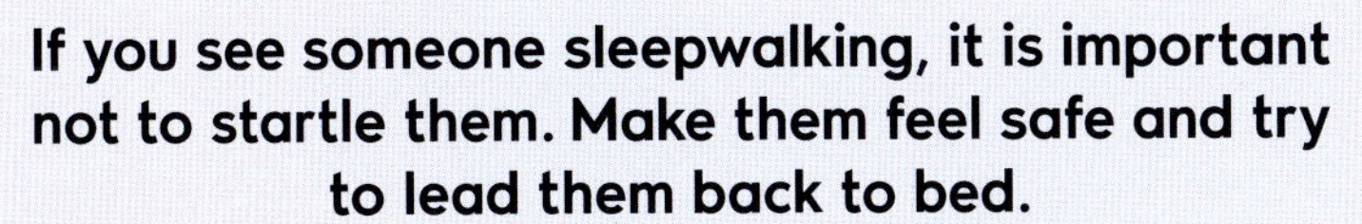

If you see someone sleepwalking, it is important not to startle them. Make them feel safe and try to lead them back to bed.

People usually grow out of sleepwalking.

Wetting the Bed

Sometimes we can wet the bed. This can happen in phase three of sleep.

We might be so deeply asleep that we don't realize we need to pee—and we might even dream we are going to the bathroom!

If you wet the bed often, try not to drink water an hour before bedtime and make sure you pee before going to bed.

Sleepy Stats

Five minutes after waking up, you will have forgotten around half of your dream.

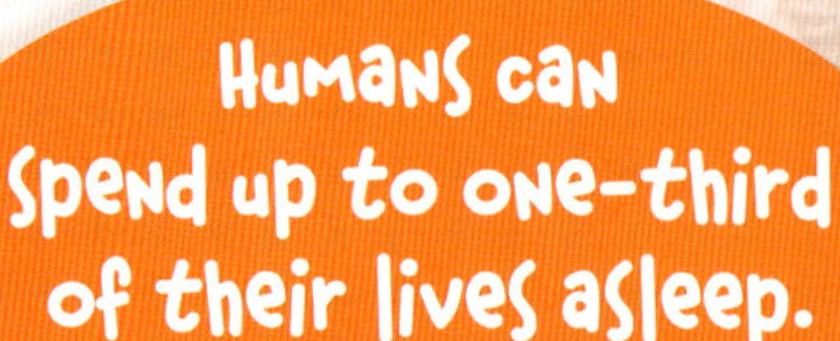

Humans can spend up to one-third of their lives asleep.

Test Your Knowledge

Match the picture to the right phase of sleep! Check back through the book if you can't remember.

A.

B.

C.

D.

Answers: A. Phase 3; B. Phase 3; C. Phase 4; D. Phase 1

Glossary

evolution: the process by which living things develop over time

immune system: the system that our body uses to defend itself against illness

muscles: bundles of tissue that can contract or squeeze together

oxygen: a natural gas that most living things need in order to survive

repairs: fixes or mends

temperature: how hot or cold something is

vibrate: to move up and down, left and right, or back and forward very fast

vivid: clear or bright

Index

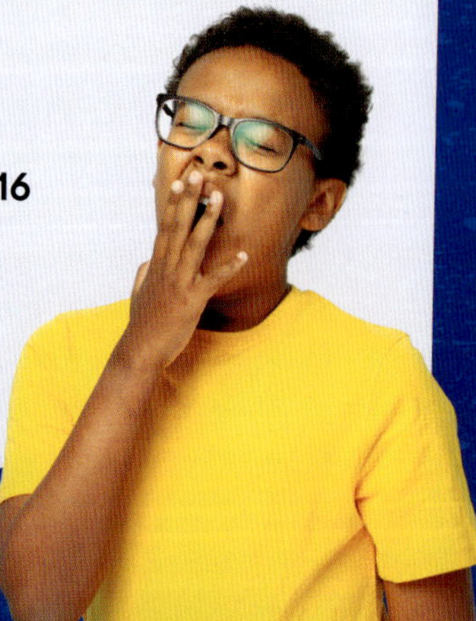

Recharging
Recharging
Recharging

Recharging
Recharging